W9-CUW-473

Sense of Place
Landscapes

by Leo Thomson

A⁺
Smart Apple Media

First published in 2005 by Hodder Wayland
338 Euston Road, London NW1 3BH, United Kingdom
Hodder Wayland is an imprint of Hodder Children's Books, a
division of Hodder Headline Limited.

Series Concept: Ruth Thomson, Series Consultant: Erika
Langmuir, Editor and Picture Research: Margot Richardson,
Designers: Rachel Hamdi and Holly Mann

The publishers would like to thank the following for
permission to reproduce their pictures:
Page 1 © National Gallery Collection; By kind permission
of the Trustees of the National Gallery, London/CORBIS;
4 © Georgia O'Keeffe, ARS, NY, and DACS, London 2003,
Provenance: Museo Thyssen-Bornemisza; 5 © ADAGP, Paris and
DACS, London 2003, National Gallery of Art, Washington,
D.C., Lauros/Giraudon/Bridgeman Art Library/
www.bridgeman.co.uk; 6 Wallace Collection, London,
UK/www.bridgeman.co.uk; 7 Tate, London 2004;
8-9 © National Gallery Collection; By kind permission
of the Trustees of the National Gallery, London/CORBIS;
11 Alte Pinakothek, Munich, Germany, Lauros/Giraudon/
Bridgeman Art Library/www.bridgeman.co.uk; 12 L&M Services
BV Amsterdam 2004057; 13 © 1986 David Hockey/The J. Paul
Getty Museum, Los Angeles; 14 © Burstein Collection/CORBIS;
15 Tate, London 2004; 16–17 © Bettmann/CORBIS; 18–19
National Gallery, London, UK/www.bridgeman.co.uk; 20 © Francis
G. Mayer/CORBIS; 21 Tate, London 2004; 22 © Copyright of
the Trustees of The British Museum; 23 National Palace
Museum, Taipei, Taiwan, Republic of China; 24 © Joseph
Stella/Yale University Art Gallery (Gift of Collection Societe
Anonyme); 25 © Tullio Crali, by kind permission of Massimo
Crali/Private Collection, Rome, Italy, Credit: Accademia Italiana,
London/www.bridgeman.co.uk; 26 The Zimmerman Family
Collection, photo © John Bigelow Taylor; 27 © Jerry Uelsmann.

Published in the United States by Smart Apple Media
2140 Howard Drive West, North Mankato, Minnesota 56003

Library of Congress Cataloging-in-Publication Data

Thomson, Leo.
Sense of place: landscapes / by Leo Thomson.
p. cm. — (Artventure)
Includes index.
ISBN 1-58340-622-0
1. Landscape in art—Juvenile literature. I. Title. II. Series.

N8213.T478 2005
758'.1—dc22   2004059018

9 8 7 6 5 4 3 2 1

Contents

Words in **bold** can be found in the glossary

Looking at landscapes

Georgia O'Keeffe, **From the Plains II**, *1954*

Landscape is the space that surrounds us outdoors. It is where earth and sky, night and day, nature and people meet. Artists have pictured landscapes from around the world at various times of day, in all types of weather, and in every season. They have painted local scenes, faraway places, and landscapes they see only in their dreams.

A window to the world

Artists share with us what they see, think, and feel in the space of the landscape. A picture can **immerse** us in the **sensation** of a place. A landscape can be a window to another world, making us think of being outside in nature even when we are inside a building in a city.

A sense of place and space

Georgia O'Keeffe was a 20th-century American artist. She lived in the New Mexican desert and often painted outside in the wilderness. This painting (left) captures her feeling of being in the vast, wild expanse of the American plains, under the fiery glow of the sunlit sky.

• How do you know when you are looking at a picture and not the real world?

• Which frames are landscape and which are portrait in the picture below?

Framing a scene

The **shape** of a picture frames the view we see in it. Pictures that are taller than they are wide are called "portrait." Pictures that are wider than they are tall are called "landscape," although a picture of a landscape can be any shape.

Magritte was a Belgian painter who lived from 1898 to 1967. His painting has three **frames**: the edges of the canvas on the easel, the window frame, and the edges of the picture itself. Magritte makes us aware of the frames, letting us see the scene as if we were both inside and outside at the same time.

❏ René Magritte
The Human Condition
1933

5

The grand landscape

❏ Peter Paul Rubens, **Landscape with a Rainbow**, *1636*

Artists have often pictured people in the natural environment to show their relationship to the earth.

Life on Earth

Rubens, a **Flemish** artist, painted this **idyllic** scene showing people living in peace with the natural world, enjoying the fruits of the earth. On an autumn afternoon, with the sun low in the sky, farmers harvest the season's crops.

Rainbow of life

In the Bible, the rainbow is a **symbol** of God's promise to let life flourish in its many different ways on Earth. Here, the rainbow ties the color and space of the picture together and guides our eye across the scene. We see the landscape spreading far into the distance, giving a sense of the **expanse** of the world.

❑ John Martin
The Great Day of His Wrath
1851–53

▲ The scene is lit by the dramatic light of fire and lightning.

▲ A whole city is thrown into the air and falls back to Earth.

▲ The land rises on each side, trapping us in the scene.

• What qualities make a landscape peaceful or terrifying?

• What differences in color, light, and shape can you see in these two pictures?

The end of the world

Here, man is at the mercy of nature, as the earth spits fire, mountains crumble, and lightning strikes. Martin, a 19th-century British painter, tells the story of the end of the world, brought about by God's anger at mankind. Martin uses the trembling figures in the **foreground** to show the terror of the situation and the awesome sense of the **scale** of the scene.

Here I stand

☐ Meindert Hobbema, **The Avenue at Middleharnis**, *1689*

It seems as if we could walk right into this picture and along the country road. We feel as if we are there, looking far into the distance, even though we are looking at a flat painting. The artist has created this **illusion** of space by using the technique of **perspective**, a way of showing three-dimensional space in a flat picture.

Flat space

The picture is like a window to the scene, as if the rays of light seen through the window turned to paint on its surface. The space contained in the scene is flattened on the **canvas**, so when we look at the picture, the scene seems to spread out far behind the painting itself.

Deep space

The picture mimics the way we see the world. Objects that are farther away appear smaller and smaller until they disappear into the distance. Things in the distance appear paler, as if we are seeing them through miles of air.

- When you look around you, how do you know how far away things are?
- Why do things change in appearance as you move around them?

Our viewpoint

When we look at this picture, we see the scene from a particular **viewpoint**. It is as if we are standing in the middle of the road, looking at the scene before us.

The horizon

The farthest we can see is the **horizon**, where the earth and sky appear to meet. The horizon is as far as we can see around Earth's curve.

The vanishing point

On the horizon, the sides of the road appear to meet and vanish. This is the **vanishing point** of the picture, or the farthest we can see on the path. Everything in the picture shrinks in size toward this point.

Time to meet

In the distance, a man with a dog is walking toward us. We know we will meet him eye to eye walking on the path, since his head appears in our line of sight. This creates an expectation of the future, pulling us into a journey along the avenue.

Window of time

Looking at the picture, we have no way of knowing whether or not the scene existed. We believe in it because it looks real. In fact, the picture is a very accurate **re-creation** of a view in south Holland that has hardly changed since Hobbema painted it in 1689. His artistic skill transports us to this distant time and place.

◻ Meindert Hobbema, **The Avenue at Middleharnis**, *1689*

◀ The sky seems to slope down to the horizon.

◀ The trees shrink in size toward the vanishing point.

◀ The barn stretches toward the vanishing point.

◀ The horizon is low in the frame, making us feel close to the ground.

◀ The road narrows to the vanishing point.

- Why can't we see all the way around Earth?
- How different would things look if we had the viewpoint of a bird in the air?

A global perspective

A perspective view can connect the things we see near us with the wide expanse of Earth.

A changing world

This picture shows history in the making: the victory of Greek leader Alexander the Great over the **Persians** in 334 B.C. Altdorfer, a German artist working in the 16th century, set the battle within a vast landscape of earth, water, and sky to express this epic struggle and the battle's huge impact on the world.

A cosmic view

The picture uses an all-embracing perspective to connect people, mountains, sea, and sky. Our bird's-eye view rises from the action of the battle in the foreground up into the air, revealing more and more landscape, until we see Earth's curve.

Universal time

The picture captures more than an **instant** in time. We see the sun and the moon, day and night together. On the ground below, the **chaos** of battle stretches through days and nights.

A world in the eye

The picture creates a whole world for our eyes to roam, following the great detail of the scene. The vertical frame emphasizes the connection between the earth and the sky, revealing the worlds of both humans and the heavens at once.

Time of life

Altdorfer was an architect and a politician, as well as a painter. He declined the position of mayor in his town, Regensburg, so as to have time to complete this monumental painting.

The life of a painting

The painting became famous only hundreds of years after it was painted. In 1800, Napoleon's army carried it from Munich to Paris, where Napoleon is said to have kept it in his bathroom. It was later exhibited in the Louvre in Paris and has now finally returned to Munich.

- How high would we have to fly to see all of Earth at once?
- Is it unusual to see the sun and the moon together in the sky?

◀ The clouds seem to part for the tablet recording the battle.

◀ The tassel points to Alexander chasing Darius, the Persian leader, who flees on his chariot.

◀ The battle is lit by the dramatic red glow of the sunset.

◀ The horizon is high in the picture, making us feel high in the air.

◀ The swarms of soldiers guide our eye around the scene.

◀ At the bottom of the picture, we are near the ground and feel close to the action.

❏ Albrecht Altdorfer
Battle of Issus, *1529*
Issus was an ancient town in Asia Minor (modern-day Turkey).

Multiple perspectives

When we are in a space, we move our eyes to see in all directions and walk around to get different viewpoints. A picture with a single, **static** viewpoint cannot capture all of these movements.

All at once

Cubism is a way of painting with multiple viewpoints, all shown at the same time, capturing a scene from all angles and giving a sense of motion in time. This painting shows the Eiffel Tower in Paris as seen both from the ground upward and from a dizzying height in the clouds. There is no horizon or vanishing point, so we feel as if we are floating in space.

❑ Robert Delaunay
Tour Eiffel 1910 (Eiffel Tower)
1911
In 1911, Paris was the center of the artistic world, and the Eiffel Tower was its symbol of modern city life and technological skill.

❏ David Hockney
**Pearlblossom Hwy.,
11–18th April, 1986 #2**
1986

A wandering viewpoint

Hockney is a contemporary artist who is interested in art that takes time to make and time to look at. He spent nine days walking around the desert in California, taking photographs from different viewpoints, some from down low and some from the top of a ladder. Hockney had the photos printed at his local photo lab, then spent two weeks in his studio carefully composing more than 500 of them into this **collage**. The result is a record of his time spent indoors as well as outdoors in the landscape. The finished picture looks as if it has one central viewpoint. In fact, it has many, creating a view you could never see in real life.

• Why does it take time to experience space?

Texture of the elements

Landscape is made of natural **elements**: earth, water, fire, air, and space. But pictures are made of paint, ink, or other materials. Artists use these materials to re-create nature's qualities in their work, using their own language of color, **texture**, and **form**.

Calm storm

Japanese artist Hokusai sets a violent storm against the quiet mass of Mount Fuji. He freezes the moment of a lightning strike with sharp, **abstract** shapes. In the distance, the colored tones of earth, water, and sky blend to evoke the drifting, storm-filled air.

❏ Hokusai
Mount Fuji Above the Lightning
1829–33

The picture is a woodcut print, made by carefully cutting out lines in a block of wood, then inking the block to print on paper. This is an ancient technique used to make thousands of pictures from a single drawing.

Storm of paint

In this painting by Turner, a British artist, the paint *is* the storm. The paint blows like the wind, washes like the sea, and drives like the snow. Turner claimed that he was tied to the mast of a ship to experience the storm. He re-created the movement and energy of the storm on the canvas, mixing his paint into the continuous whirl of water moving between sea and sky. All we see is water. There is no horizon, and our view is tilted as if we are aboard the swaying ship.

- What makes water look wet?
- Could you draw water with any materials you liked?

❑ J. M. W. Turner
Snowstorm: Steamboat off a Harbor's Mouth
1842

Earthly paradise

A picture can evoke the atmosphere of a time and place, whether real or **imaginary**.

Urban paradise

Here Seurat, a French artist, pictures the River Seine in Paris as an Earthly paradise. Nature provides a gentle and peaceful place of leisure. The Parisians simply gaze upon the world. The day shimmers with the heat and color of summer, and the vitality of nature fills every inch of the canvas. The surface is carefully painted with an **intricate** pattern of color, suggesting the endless variety of natural forms.

▲ Long shadows suggest the afternoon sun.

▲The people have glowing halos of light around their heads.

▲Dark, shadowy areas make the sunlit areas seem brighter.

▲The dog is frozen in mid-leap, capturing the stillness of an instant.

❏ Georges Seurat **Sunday Afternoon on the Island of La Grande Jatte**, *1884–86*

Particles of color

Seurat painted with millions of individual dots of color. He developed this technique, called pointillism, based on the scientific theory of his time. The dots of color mix in the eye when seen from a distance but keep their own individual brilliance.

Complementary colors

Pairs of complementary colors placed together look more brilliant than colors on their own. Seurat used a version of a color wheel (see above) to calculate which colors are complementary and placed these next to each other on the canvas, creating millions of color contrasts in the scene.

Color of time

The painting has the warm orange glow of a summer afternoon. Everything has both its own color and specks of color from the things around it. Seurat added tiny specks of orange for the sunlight falling on the scene.

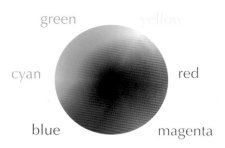

Color wheel

Seurat used tiny dots of complementary colors to create a vivid and brilliant effect.

❏ Georges Seurat
Sunday Afternoon on the Island of La Grande Jatte
(details)

◀Today, we know that the human eye can see more than seven million different colors. Artists can mix most of these from just three **primary colors**: red, yellow, and blue.

◀Pairs of colors opposite each other on the wheel are complementary colors: yellow and blue, red and cyan, magenta and green. Any two complementary colors mixed together will make dull, grayish tones, but put side by side, they seem dazzlingly bright.

An ideal moment

This painting occupied Seurat for almost two years. He visited the island every day for months, making studies of the landscape. He also had models pose in his studio. He put all of this together to create an imaginary moment in time.

An eternal instant

The picture forms a world of delicate **harmony** and variety, the fleeting qualities of an instant. Seurat gives the moment such grandeur that it lasts in the mind like a memory, taking on a life of its own.

Wild vision

☐ Vincent van Gogh
Cornfield with Cypresses
1889

▲ Complementary blues
and yellows give the scene
a heat-struck intensity.

▲ The shrubs in the
foreground give a sense of
depth to the field.

▲ The tall cypress trees,
associated with cemeteries
and death, are dark figures
in the scene.

❏ Vincent van Gogh
Cornfield with Cypresses (detail)
The clouds are painted with thick brush strokes, giving a sense of their bulk and weight compared with the thin, blue sky.

Our state of mind changes the way we see the world. A picture can give shape to an artist's thoughts and moods, sharing with us his or her unique vision of life.

Nature of the mind

In this picture, Dutch painter Vincent van Gogh captures the ever-changing energy of nature. He gives everything a wild and shifting form. Each brush stroke is thick and distinct, giving weight and volume to the forms of plants, rocks, and sky. Every mark is different, shaped by the changing flow of van Gogh's thoughts.

Color in a tube

The **vivid** colors of the painting come from the bright, ready-made paints that van Gogh's brother regularly sent him from Paris. These newly invented paints let van Gogh work quickly, on his own, and outdoors without having to worry about mixing his colors from **pigments**.

Fragile nature

Van Gogh saw the world with extreme intensity and painted it so. He was often mentally unstable and is famous for cutting off his earlobe.

He continued to paint even when admitted to the hospital for mental illness. This picture was painted near the hospital in St-Rémy-de-Provence, France, where he spent a year at the end of his life.

• Do any two clouds in the sky ever take exactly the same shape?

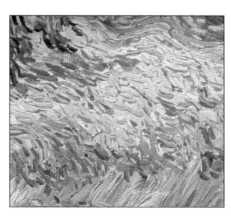

❏ Vincent van Gogh
Cornfield with Cypresses (detail)
The wheat is painted with very thick paint, like a layer of tiny sculptures on the canvas.

Scenes and stories

A landscape can tell a story, **evoking** the past, present, and future of a scene all at the same time.

Fateful future

This picture is like a moment in a movie: we wonder what will happen next. The forces of nature have created the drama. The wind and the waves have destroyed the boat's mast and sails, leaving it drifting on the currents. Now, hungry sharks circle the boat. There is blood in the water, and a **tornado** looms on the horizon, threatening the lone sailor with death. We cannot be sure if the tornado will pass or if the ship in the distance might come to the rescue. We are left to watch the sailor think about his uncertain future.

❏ Winslow Homer, **The Gulf Stream**, *1889*

Paul Nash, in the top right of the image.

❑ Paul Nash, **We are Making a New World**, *1918*

Silent land

Paul Nash was a British soldier and war artist during World War I. He **sketched** this scene of devastation on the front line in France and painted it on his return to England. The scene is empty of people, suggesting a battle with no survivors.

The landscape itself tells the story. The sun passes behind red clouds, suggesting the blood of war. The land has been churned up by battle, and the trees are burned to their cores. However, the sun is perhaps a symbol of hope in the scene, as it still rises and sets, and the cycles of life go on.

Slow landscapes

Natural form changes all the time. Looking closely, we can become lost in its details.

War and peace

This scene, part of a book painted by Sultan Muhammad in Persia in the 16th century, pictures a hero, Rustam, asleep in the forest while his horse battles a lion. The warrior rests at peace, surrounded by the lush beauty of the forest. A rich patchwork of colors and styles captures the variety of life. The clouds twirl and even the rocks seem alive. The scene just piles up, without any strict perspective, giving everything a strange scale. The free **composition** and loose borders let the individual parts flourish, and the text floats through the scene.

❏ Sultan Muhammad (attributed to)
Rustam Sleeps while Rakhsh Fights Off a Lion
1515–22

Timeless space

Fan Kuan, an 11th-century artist, lived in the mountains of Shansi, China. His picture takes our eyes on a journey through the landscape, following the path as it climbs up the mountains from the valley. We see far more of the landscape than we could ever see at one time from any one viewpoint. Misty clouds hide the path and the horizon, suggesting an unknown space and time between the mountains. The scene has been left unfinished, letting us complete the landscape and our journey in our mind.

• Can a picture ever really be complete and describe all of a landscape?

❏ Fan Kuan
Scholar Pavilion in the Cloudy Mountain, Song Dynasty
11th century

23

Fast landscapes

Joseph Stella
**Battle of Lights,
Coney Island, Mardi Gras**
1913–14

▲ The shapes and colors pile up like hundreds of sensations felt at once.

▲ The **silhouettes** of dancers blend with abstract forms to make a writhing sea of life.

▲ The steel girders of the roller coaster tangle up with all of the action.

24

Our **technology** changes the landscape. We make the world bright with electric lights, noisy with speeding cars and planes, and warmer with all of our activity. Artists have expressed this **frantic** modern landscape with intense, **dynamic** images.

Speeding space

Joseph Stella, an Italian-American painting in the early 20th century, depicts a man-made landscape throbbing with electricity (left). The lights, noise, and speed of the carnival collapse into a whirl of shape and color. There is no single moment in time or viewpoint in space. All of the sensations of the night come together in a seething mass of rhythm and form to make an abstract, modern world.

- How does electricity change our landscape?
- How does a scene look different when viewed from a moving car or plane?

❏ Tullio Crali
Dogfight
1936–38

Spinning world

The painting above captures the sweeping, curling path of a plane in a single, speeding image. The ground spins as we loop the loop with the pilot. The plane's movement warps his view of the earth, curving the horizon and turning the world upside down.

25

Landscapes of the mind

Artists can use the elements of landscape to portray fantastical visions of strange, alternative realities.

Inner worlds

This picture is a mandala, or a **diagram** made by **Buddhists** to show the inner forces of the **universe**. It expresses the connection between the inner world of the mind and the outer world of the environment.

Order and chaos

At the center is a small triangle of calm with a symbol of a goddess, which is surrounded by a terrifying world of blood and fire. The man-made shapes of the square, circle, and triangle contrast with the wild forms of the seething ocean and raging flames.

The world seems balanced between order and chaos, each existing within the other.

▲The blue triangle seems to float in an endless universe of fire.

▲The human figure forms a whole continent in the middle of a red ocean. Within his body is an inner mandala of **symmetrical** forms.

❑ Unknown artist
Geluk Order, Tibet
Fire Mandala
17th–18th century

▼ Try placing a mirror along the center line to see how the image is symmetrical.

◀ The trees float free of gravity, as if on another planet.

◀ The tree roots are a photograph of a leafless winter tree turned upside down. The combined tree has both its summer and winter form.

◀ The seed pod is a symbol of natural reproduction and the cycles of birth and death.

❏ Jerry Uelsmann, **Floating Tree**, *1969*

Human nature

This photograph plays with nature to create an unearthly **reality**. The land on the left is a mirror image of that on the right, and two identical trees float above the scene, their roots free of the earth. The artist shows a strange, intelligent nature dividing and multipliying to reproduce itself.

Uelsmann, an American artist, takes photos of real landscapes and plays with them in the **darkroom**, carefully combining many images to make a single print. He does not use computers to alter images, preferring the mystery of darkness and chemical reactions. He creates a nature of the mind, exploring the mysterious workings of the world and our thoughts.

About the artists

The symbols below show the size and shape of the works shown in this book compared with an average-sized adult.

Albrecht ALTDORFER (page 11)

(1480–1538) German
Battle of Issus, 1529
Oil on panel, 62.2 x 47.2 inches
(158 x 120 cm)
Alte Pinakothek, Munich, Germany

Other landscapes
❏ *Landscape with Castle*, 1522–25
   Alte Pinakothek, Munich, Germany
❏ *Willow Landscape*, 1511
   Akedemie der Bildenden Kunste, Vienna, Austria

Tullio CRALI (page 25)

(1910–2000) Italian
Dogfight, 1936–38
Oil on cardboard, 39.4 x 43.3 inches (100 x 110 cm)
Private Collection

Other landscapes
❏ *Nose Dive on the City*, 1939
   Private Collection
❏ *The Force of the Curve*, 1930
   Private Collection

Robert DELAUNAY (page 12)

(1885–1941) French
Tour Eiffel 1910 (Eiffel Tower), 1911
Oil on canvas, 79.5 x 54.5 inches (201.9 x 138.4 cm)
Solomon R. Guggenheim Museum, New York

Other landscapes
❏ *Circular Forms*, 1930
   Solomon R. Guggenheim Museum, New York
❏ *Simultaneous Contrasts: Sun and Moon*, 1913
   The Museum of Modern Art, New York

Vincent van GOGH (pages 18–19)

(1853–1890) Dutch
Cornfield with Cypresses, 1889
Oil on Canvas, 28.5 x 36 inches (72.5 x 91.5 cm)
National Gallery, London, UK

Other landscapes
❏ *Starry Night*, 1889
   Metropolitan Museum of Art, New York
❏ *Field Under Thunderclouds*, 1890
   Vincent van Gogh Foundation, Amsterdam, Holland

Meindert HOBBEMA (pages 8–9)

(1638–1709) Dutch
The Avenue at Middleharnis, 1689
Oil on canvas, 40.7 x 55.5 inches (103.5 x 141 cm)
The National Gallery, London, UK

Other landscapes
❏ *Woodland Road*, 1670
   The Metropolitan Museum of Art, New York
❏ *A Wooded Landscape*, 1667
   J. Paul Getty Museum, Los Angeles, California

David HOCKNEY (page 13)

(1937–) British
Pearlblossom Hwy., 11–18th April, 1986, #2, 1986
Photographic collage, 78 x 111 inches (198 x 282 cm)
The J. Paul Getty Museum, Los Angeles, California

Other landscapes
❏ *A Walk Around the Hotel Courtyard, Acatlan*, 1985
   Andre Emmerich Gallery, New York
❏ *The Brooklyn Bridge*, 1982
   Private collection

HOKUSAI (page 14)

(1760–1849) Japanese
Mount Fuji Above the Lightning, 1829–33
Woodcut print, 10.2 x 15 inches (25.9 x 38.2 cm)
Musée Guimet, Paris, France

Other landscapes

❏ *The Great Wave off Kanagawa*, 1830–31
   The Metropolitan Museum of Art, New York
❏ *A Sudden Gust of Wind at Ejri*, 1831
   Musée Guimet, Paris, France

Winslow HOMER (page 20)

(1836–1910) American
The Gulf Stream, 1889
Oil on canvas, 28.1 x 49.1 inches (71.4 x 124.8 cm)
The Metropolitan Museum of Art, New York

Other landscapes

❏ *Moonlight, Wood Island Night*, 1894
   The Metropolitan Museum of Art, New York
❏ *A Summer Night*, 1890
   Palais de Alma, Paris, France
❏ *Kissing the Moon*, 1904
   Addison Gallery of American Art, Massachusetts

Fan KUAN (page 23)

(10th–early 11th century) Chinese
Scholar Pavillon in the Cloudy Mountain, Song Dynasty, 11th century
Ink on Silk
National Palace Museum, Taipei, Taiwan, Republic of China

Other landscapes

❏ *Travelers Among Mountains and Streams*, 11th century
   National Palace Museum, Taipei, Taiwan, Republic of China
❏ *Winter Landscape with Temples and Travelers*, 11th century
   Museum of Fine Arts, Boston

René MAGRITTE (page 5)

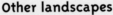

(1898–1967) Belgian
The Human Condition, 1933
Oil on Canvas, 31.8 x 39.6 inches (80.7 x 100.6 cm)
Private Collection

Other landscapes

❏ *Golconda*, 1953
   Private collection
❏ *The Empire of Lights*, 1958
   Private Collection
❏ *Free hand*, 1965
   National Gallery of Art, Washington, D.C.

John MARTIN (page 7)

(1789–1854) British
The Great Day of His Wrath, 1851–53
Oil on Canvas, 77.4 x 119.4 inches (196.5 x 303.2 cm)
Tate Britain, London, UK

Other landscapes

❏ *The Last Judgement*, 1853
   Tate Britain, London, UK
❏ *The Plains of Heaven*, 1853
   Tate Britain, London, UK

Sultan MUHAMMAD (attributed to, page 22)

(15th–16th century) Iranian (Tabriz)
Rustam Sleeps while Rakhsh Fights Off a Lion, 1515–22
Page from a manuscript of the Shahnama (Book of Kings), Gouache on paper, 16.1 x 11.5 inches (40.8 x 29.3 cm)
British Museum, London, UK

Other landscapes

❏ *The Court of Gayumars*, from The Shah Tahmasp Shamana of Firdausi, 1522–25
   Collection of Prince and Princess Sadruddin Aga Kahn
❏ Pages from *Gulistan of Sa'di*, 1525–30
   Keir Collection

Paul NASH (page 21)

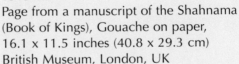

(1889–1946) British
We Are Making a New World, 1918
Oil on Canvas, 28.1 x 36 inches (71.4 x 91.4 cm)
Imperial War Museum, London, UK

Other landscapes

❏ *The Menin Road*, 1918–19
   Imperial War Museum, London, UK
❏ *Totes Meer*, 1940–41, Tate Britain, London, UK

Georgia O'KEEFFE (page 4)

(1887–1986) American
From the Plains II, 1954
Oil on Canvas, 48 x 72 inches (122 x 183 cm)
Fundación Colleción Thyssen-Bornemisza, Madrid, Spain

Other works
❑ *Winter Road I*, 1963
National Gallery of Art, Washington, D.C.
❑ *Sky Above the Clouds I*, 1963
The Georgia O'Keeffe Museum, Santa Fe, New Mexico
❑ *Summer Days*, 1936
Whitney Museum of American Art, New York

Peter Paul RUBENS (page 6)

(1577–1640) Flemish
Landscape with a Rainbow, 1636
Oil on oak, 53.5 x 92.5 inches (136 x 235 cm)
Wallace Collection, London, UK

Other landscapes
❑ *An Autumn Landscape with a View of Het Steen in the Morning*, 1636
National Gallery, London, UK

Georges SEURAT (pages 16–17)

(1851–1891) French
Sunday Afternoon on the Island of La Grande Jatte, 1884–86
Oil on Canvas, 81.7 x 121.3 inches (207.6 x 308 cm)
The Art Institute of Chicago, Illinois

Other landscapes
❑ *Bathers at Asnières*, 1883–84
National Gallery, London, UK
❑ *La Bec Du Hoc Grandcamp*, 1885
Tate Britain, London, UK
❑ *Channel at Gravelines, Petit Fort Phillipe*, 1890
Indianapolis Museum of Art, Indiana

Joseph STELLA (page 24)

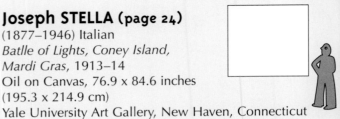

(1877–1946) Italian
Battle of Lights, Coney Island, Mardi Gras, 1913–14
Oil on Canvas, 76.9 x 84.6 inches (195.3 x 214.9 cm)
Yale University Art Gallery, New Haven, Connecticut

Other landscapes
❑ *Flowers, Italy*, 1930, Phoenix Art Museum, Arizona
❑ *Tree of My Life*, 1919–20
Mr. and Mrs. Barney A. Ebsworth Foundation and Windsor Inc., St. Louis, Missouri
❑ *New York Interpreted (The Voice of the City)*, 1920–22
The Newark Museum, New Jersey

J. M. W. TURNER (page 15)

(1775–1851) British
Snowstorm: Steamboat off a Harbor's Mouth, 1842
Oil on Canvas, 36 x 48 inches (91.4 x 121.9 cm)
Tate Britain, London, UK

Other landscapes
❑ *Hannibal and His Army Crossing The Alps*, 1812
Tate Britain, London, UK
❑ *Light and Color, Goethes Theory—The Morning After the Deluge*, 1843
Tate Liverpool, Liverpool, UK

Jerry UELSMANN (page 27)

(1934–) American
Floating Tree,1969
Gelatin Siver print, 15.7 x 19.7 inches (40 x 50 cm)
Collection of Jerry Uelsmann

Unknown artist: Geluk Order, Tibet (page 26)

Fire Mandala, 17th–18th century
Ink and watercolors on cloth,
24 x 18.5 inches (61 x 47 cm)
The Zimmerman Family Collection, New York

Other Buddhist mandalas
❑ *Kalachakra Mandala*, 17th century
Museum of Fine Arts, Boston, Massachusetts
❑ *Mandala of Six Chakravartins*, 15th century
Philadelphia Museum of Art, Pennsylvania

Glossary

Abstract Shapes and forms not shown in a real way.

Buddhists People who follow Buddhism, a religion from India.

Canvas A piece of coarse, stretched cloth on which artists often paint.

Chaos Complete disorder and confusion.

Collage An artwork made of many pieces stuck together.

Composition The organization of the parts of a picture.

Darkroom A completely darkened room for developing film and photographs.

Diagram A simplified drawing that shows how things work.

Dynamic Full of energy, movement, or change.

Elements Basic parts.

Evoking Calling up in the mind.

Expanse A wide stretch.

Flemish From Flanders, a place that is now divided between Belgium, France, and the Netherlands.

Foreground The part of a painting that seems closest to the viewer.

Form The complete three-dimensional shape of an object.

Frame A border around something.

Frantic Fast and chaotic.

Harmony A complete and balanced state.

Horizon The line where Earth's surface and the sky appear to meet.

Idyllic Blissful or peaceful.

Illusion A false or unreal picture, idea, or belief.

Imaginary Something only in the mind.

Immerse Put in completely.

Instant A particular moment of time.

Intricate Finely detailed.

Persians People from a place called Persia (now known as Iran).

Perspective A method of painting or drawing landscapes, figures, and objects to make them appear three-dimensional.

Pigments The colors in paint.

Primary colors Red, yellow, and blue—pure colors that cannot be made by mixing other colors together.

Re-creation Something that has been created again.

Reality What really exists, rather than what is imagined.

Scale The relative size of things.

Sensation A feeling our senses give us.

Shape The form or outline of someone or something.

Silhouettes Shapes or forms shown only as an outline.

Sketched Drawn quickly or roughly. (Sketches are often done as a guide for a more detailed painting.)

Static Without movement, action, or change.

Symbol Something that stands for something else.

Symmetrical Made of parts that are a mirror image of each other.

Technology The use of science for practical purposes.

Texture The feel and appearance of a surface.

Tornado A funnel-shaped cloud that is made by violently circling winds and touches earth.

Universe Everything that exists.

Vanishing point The point at which parallel lines going back appear to join in the distance.

Viewpoint The place our eyes would be to see a scene in a painting or other work of art.

Vivid Intensely deep or bright.

Index